PREPARING FOR DISASTER

ENGINEERING SOLUTIONS FOR

EPIDEMICS AND PANDEMICS

D1518049

KARA ROGERS

rosen publishing's
**rosen
central**

New York

Published in 2020 by The Rosen Publishing Group, Inc.
29 East 21st Street, New York, NY 10010

Copyright © 2020 by The Rosen Publishing Group, Inc.

First Edition

Library of Congress Cataloging-in-Publication Data

Names: Rogers, Kara, author. Title: Engineering solutions for epidemics and pandemics / Kara Rogers.
Description: First edition. I New York: Rosen Publishing, 2020. I Series: Preparing for disaster I Audience: Grades 5 to 8 I Includes bibliographical references and index.
Identifiers: LCCN 2019008487I ISBN 9781725347793 (library bound) I ISBN 9781725347786 (pbk.)
Subjects: LCSH: Epidemics—Prevention—Juvenile literature. I Disaster medicine—Juvenile literature. I Emerging infectious diseases—Juvenile literature. I Emergency management—Juvenile literature. I Communicable diseases—Prevention—Juvenile literature. I World health—Forecasting—Juvenile literature.
Classification: LCC RA653.5 .R64 2020 I DDC 614.4—dc23 LC record available at https://lccn.loc.gov/2019008487

Manufactured in the United States of America

CONTENTS

Introduction

Throughout history, outbreaks of disease, in which an illness appears suddenly in a community, have had a strong effect on humans. The illness often is contagious, meaning that it is easily spread from one person to another. Outbreaks quickly can become widespread. They affect many people and can develop into an epidemic. If the disease continues to spread through a country or expands to other parts of the world, the outbreak becomes known as a pandemic.

Although many people may become sick because of an epidemic or a pandemic, many of these outbreaks claim very few lives. There are some diseases, however, that are more dangerous. They cause many people to become severely ill and result in many deaths as they spread through communities. Historically, outbreaks of disease often caused hundreds or even thousands of deaths. Outbreaks usually lasted two or three years, with the disease appearing again in nearby places. One of the deadliest outbreaks in modern history was the influenza pandemic of 1918 to 1919, also known as the Spanish influenza pandemic. This pandemic caused about twenty-five million deaths.

It's frightening to imagine a rapidly spreading sickness that could cause death. But medical professionals, health workers, scientists, and emergency responders are prepared. These different groups of experts carefully plan ahead. They make use of science, technology, engineering, and

A researcher works with dangerous viruses in a laboratory. Some viruses cause deadly diseases that can spread rapidly.

mathematics (STEM). They bring together tools, resources, and experience. Resources and tools include vaccines, medicines, and other approaches to treating and preventing illness. These experts know a lot about disease and how to stop people from becoming sick. They also have the skills they need to get along and share ideas with others. In this way, emergency responders, medical workers, and even individuals can work together to limit or prevent outbreaks.

CHAPTER ONE

Killer Diseases

Every year, human societies are attacked by outbreaks of disease. Long ago, people believed such outbreaks were the result of supernatural forces, such as the anger of God. Later, people blamed them on miasma, or bad air. Some people believed that by just breathing this air, they would fall ill. With the discovery in the nineteenth century of infectious microorganisms—very tiny living things that can be seen only with a microscope—a scientific understanding of disease formed. Knowing how diseases surface, how they progress, and how they can be stopped is critical to engineering solutions to epidemics and pandemics.

Diseases That Raise the Alarm

Different diseases have the ability to appear suddenly and affect many people. Some are more likely to give rise to epidemics and pandemics. Of these, there are about fifteen to twenty that experts are most concerned about. One of these is influenza, which many people simply refer to as the flu. Different types of flu move through groups of humans and animals, and every now and then new types appear. Avian influenza, for example, used to be found only in birds like chickens and ducks. But in the late twentieth century, it also began to infect humans. Avian influenza causes cough, fever, headache, sore muscles, and sore throat. These symptoms are almost identical to regular flu, but avian influenza is much worse and deadlier.

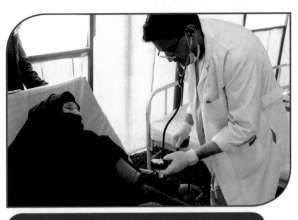

A doctor treats a patient who has been infected with cholera at a hospital in Sana'a, Yemen. Cholera causes extreme diarrhea that results in a potentially dangerous loss of water from the body.

Another disease that causes epidemics in humans is cholera. Cholera affects a part of the body called the small intestine. It causes extreme diarrhea that leads to a harmful loss of water from the body. This condition, known as dehydration, can result in death. Outbreaks of cholera have been a major concern since the 1800s. At that time, thousands of people died from cholera in places like India, Thailand, and Indonesia. It later spread to Europe and the Americas. The twenty-first century is witness to what experts call the seventh pandemic of cholera. Between 2011 and 2017, the disease caused 308 separate outbreaks. During that same time, the next two leading epidemics were of meningitis and an illness called Zika virus disease. Meningitis is caused by microscopic organisms known as bacteria. It can be a life-threatening disease. It affects the meninges, the thin membranes that cover the brain and spinal cord. Like cholera, it began to affect large numbers of people in the 1800s. The first outbreaks of meningitis took place in Europe, North America, and Africa.

Other diseases that cause epidemics include yellow fever, chickungunya fever, and West Nile fever. All three of these diseases cause fever and flu-like illness. Humans can catch these diseases

A health worker wears protective equipment while offering a drink to a young Ebola patient in Sierra Leone in 2014. Africa experienced one of the worst Ebola outbreaks in history in 2014 and 2015.

from mosquitoes. Plague, shigellosis, typhoid fever, and Ebola are other important causes of epidemics. Ebola virus disease is especially alarming in humans. It spreads easily and has a high fatality rate, causing many people who catch it to die. The largest Ebola outbreak took place in 2014 to 2015 in western Africa. It mainly struck people in Guinea, Sierra Leone, and Liberia. More than 28,600 cases and 11,300 deaths were recorded by the World Health Organization (WHO).

Deadly Agents

The diseases that give rise to epidemics and pandemics typically are caused by microscopic agents, or pathogens, that infect the body.

Epidemic Versus Pandemic: What's the Difference

The terms "outbreak," "epidemic," and "pandemic" are sometimes used in place of one another. However, each of these terms has its own meaning. It is important to remember these differences especially when talking about diseases. A disease outbreak is defined as the sudden appearance of a disease or illness in a group of individuals. Epidemics and pandemics are types of outbreaks. An epidemic is a sudden occurrence of disease in which the number of cases is more than what is normal for the affected group. A pandemic basically is an epidemic but on a much larger scale. It occurs over a broad area, such as across multiple large countries or worldwide.

For this reason, these diseases commonly are described by the term "infectious disease." Pathogens include bacteria, fungi, helminths (worms), protozoa, and viruses. Of these, bacteria and viruses are the most common causes.

Once in the body, many infectious agents begin to secrete, or give off, toxins that harm cells. These toxins can enter the bloodstream, which carries them to other parts of the body. This process explains why illnesses like the flu, which mainly affects the parts of the body used for breathing, also makes the whole body ache. As infection sets in, the body begins to produce substances called antibodies that are made to kill the infectious agent. Antibodies are made by the immune system, the body's main defense against illness. The immune system usually wipes out infections, and the person begins to feel better. But sometimes it loses the battle, which can result in life-threatening illness.

Pathogens that cause infections may stay in the body for a long time. This lasting infection can happen even when a person seems

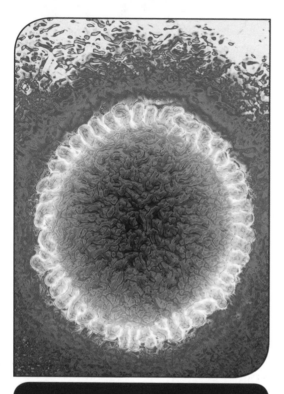

This microscopic image shows an influenza virus. The virus particle measures a mere 80 to 120 nanometers across (1 nanometer = 0.0000001 centimeter).

to have gotten over an illness and is feeling better. Pathogens that hang around may cause a person to have flare-ups of sickness later, or they may develop other chronic, or long-term, symptoms. It may take many months to get over this type of infection. Thankfully, some infections can be prevented ahead of time. The easiest way to prevent infection is with a vaccine. A vaccine is a preparation of a weakened or killed infectious agent or its toxin. Vaccines do not cause infections. Rather, they tell the immune system to produce antibodies that give immunity, or protection, against deadly diseases.

Most infectious agents are host specific. This term means that they cause disease in just one or several closely related kinds of animals. For example, some agents infect only birds, while others infect only humans and other primates, such as monkeys. This circumstance explains why people become sick but their pet cat or dog usually does not. However, one of the most feared things about infectious agents is that many of them evolve, or change. Over time, this change results in new types of agents. Because the human body has not seen these new forms before, they tend to cause very bad illness.

Infectious agents change in many ways. But of special concern is their ability to "jump" between species. For example, the HIV virus that causes AIDS, a disease that spread in humans worldwide beginning in the 1980s, is thought to have come from a virus that infects apes and monkeys. Humans probably caught this virus when African hunters who used chimpanzees and other primates for food touched the animals' blood. Once in humans, the virus probably changed. Today it exists in a form that causes long-term illness in humans.

Flashback: Tracking the Cause of London's 1853 to 1854 Cholera Outbreak

From 1853 to 1854, the city of London, England, suffered its third major outbreak of cholera in only two decades. The source of the outbreaks was a mystery. But British doctor John Snow had a hunch that they were related to polluted water. To explore his idea, Snow came up with a method to track the source of disease. In his first study, he used graphs, maps, and deduction from facts to track the source of cholera to a water pump on Broad Street in London's Soho neighborhood. His second study was called the Grand Experiment. In this study, he compared water sources used by different companies that supplied water to London's neighborhoods. He showed that a company that drew water from the upper river Thames, far from the city center, had less polluted water than a second company that drew water from inlets known to be tainted by sewage in central London. The neighborhoods with water that came from farther away had fewer cases of cholera. Snow's work showed that water polluted by sewage could cause cholera. His discoveries led to the use of new strategies to make sure London's neighborhoods received clean water. These strategies helped stop future cholera outbreaks from happening in London.

Person to Person

Infectious diseases spread in different ways. Those that can be caught from a person, often through sneezing, coughing, or touching, are known as contagious diseases. Other infectious diseases are spread to humans by animals, such as ticks and mosquitoes. These diseases are not contagious, but they still can spread to enough people to give rise to an epidemic.

Some people are more likely to catch an infectious disease than others. Young children, whose immune systems are still developing, are especially at risk. Older people, who are not as strong or energetic as they used to be and who may have other health problems, are

Mosquito larvae are collected from a pool of water in California. Mosquitoes can be studied for evidence of infection with harmful agents, helping researchers track the spread of mosquito-borne diseases.

also more prone to being infected. A weak immune system, caused by an immune illness or by poor diet or stress, can make a person less able to fight off infections. Individuals who are not protected by vaccines are also more likely to catch certain illnesses.

Noninfectious Epidemics

Sometimes a disease outbreak is described as an epidemic, even though the disease that causes it is not infectious. This type of disease is called noninfectious. Epidemics of noninfectious sickness are different. They can last a long time and have unique needs to prevent and stop them.

Examples of noninfectious outbreaks include the drug-addiction and obesity epidemics in the United States. In recent years, these two epidemics have affected far more Americans than outbreaks of infectious disease. According to the 2017 National Survey on Drug Use and Health, more than two million people in the United States abused drugs called opioids. Some 47,600 of these people died from an overdose, or taking too much of these drugs. Data for 2017 also showed that about 39.6 percent of US adults and more than 18 percent of US children were obese—the greatest numbers ever in the country's history.

Epidemics of noninfectious disease also occur on smaller scales. An example is a cancer outbreak in children in Franklin, Indiana. Between 2008 and 2019, fifty-eight cases of childhood cancer had been reported in Franklin. That number was much higher than would be expected for a town its size. Investigators found cancer-causing chemicals in the ground beneath the town. The chemicals likely were left behind from industrial companies that had once operated in Franklin. One of the chemicals detected was trichloroethylene, or TCE. TCE levels were more than 252 times higher than is safe for humans. TCE can cause cancer in animals if they are around the chemical, or exposed to it, over a long time. Investigators suspect that air tainted with these chemicals is entering peoples' homes and potentially causing cancer in children.

CHAPTER TWO

Anticipating and Reacting to Disease Disasters

In the twenty-first century, the world's ability to deal with disease outbreaks has greatly improved. This development is largely because scientists now know more about disease and what can be done to stop it. Technology has also helped. Stronger, faster communication technology, for example, enables health officials worldwide to rapidly share information about where diseases are spreading.

But many factors influence the rise and spread of disease. Some examples are how healthy individuals are to begin with and what they know about disease. More and more people are also now traveling to countries all over the world where they might catch new diseases that they then bring back to their home countries. Because thinking about all these factors at once is very complex, researchers from many different areas of science and medicine work together to learn what role each factor plays in an epidemic. From this work, researchers have come up with ways to tell when an epidemic or pandemic is likely to happen and how best to react. Once an outbreak begins, courage, a swift response, and quick decision making are necessary for its defeat.

A WHO official holds a map showing the predicted worldwide distribution of the *Aedes aegypti* mosquito, a carrier of Zika virus. By early 2016, Zika virus had circulated to multiple regions in the Americas and the Caribbean, including Brazil, Puerto Rico, and Mexico.

Anticipating Epidemics

A major part of knowing how to respond to an epidemic or pandemic involves anticipation, or thinking ahead. Scientists study and learn about potential outbreak scenarios and the factors that give rise to infectious diseases. Researchers and health officials also identify certain diseases or areas of the world where epidemics and pandemics are likely to surface. By studying outbreaks that have happened before, scientists are able to better understand when and where diseases might appear next.

How Does an Epidemic Start?

Epidemics start when an infectious agent and people who might catch it come together. Usually, a large number of people must become infected for an outbreak to be considered an epidemic. Sometimes, epidemics start very suddenly, such as when an infectious agent spreads very fast through groups of people. This condition can happen when an existing agent mutates, or changes, into a form that helps it more easily infect people. In other cases, epidemics start because a new infectious agent has appeared. Because people have no immunity against it, it can quickly spread through many people. Also, the immunity of a large group of people can change over time. This situation can happen in towns or cities where growing numbers of individuals choose not to receive vaccines themselves or vaccinate their children, reducing overall immunity of the group. Infectious agents that were once held off through this so-called community immunity can reappear, causing an epidemic in unvaccinated people.

Researchers also keep a close watch on emerging, or new, infectious threats. For example, the Emerging Pandemic Threats (EPT) program, organized by the United States Agency for International Development (USAID), has strategies to find, control, and prevent infectious diseases in animals and humans. The quick identification of new infectious agents that come from animals gives researchers time to figure out how dangerous the agents are and how they can be stopped from causing harm to humans.

Watching Out for Disease

It is the job of some health experts to keep watch for when the next epidemic or pandemic might occur. This process of close

Workers unload medical supplies in Liberia during the Ebola epidemic of 2014–15. The supplies included personal protective equipment and water purification machinery, which are critical for health workers to do their job and keep the public safe.

observation forms the basis of disease surveillance. Experts in disease surveillance often work for or collaborate with international groups, such as WHO. WHO experts in disease surveillance keep health officials in countries worldwide up to date on diseases that appear to be spreading. Country leaders and health professionals use this information to prepare for and respond to outbreaks.

Keeping an eye on global trends in the spread of disease is also used to aid vaccine and medicine production. This step is especially important in the case of influenza. Flu viruses evolve quickly, with new types surfacing almost annually. Because of this rapid change, last year's flu vaccine may not protect people

Patient Zero

To better understand how an epidemic began, health workers try to trace the epidemic's history back to the first person who became sick. This person is known as patient zero, or the index case. By investigating patient zero, experts are sometimes able to find out where the disease came from and how it spread. This information can be used to guide emergency response teams. It can also be used to help stop more cases from happening.

There are several notable patient zeros from historical outbreaks. An infant living on Broad Street in London's Soho neighborhood, for example, was thought to be the first case in the 1854 cholera outbreak there. Another famous index case was Typhoid Mary. She likely carried the typhoid bacteria that caused outbreaks of typhoid fever in New York City and Long Island in the early 1900s.

against infection with this year's flu virus. Thankfully, new flu vaccines can be made quickly. Researchers in flu labs in more than one hundred different countries perform year-round influenza surveillance. Part of their job is to collect samples of flu viruses from their countries. They send these samples to larger flu research centers. Based on studies of the samples that are received by these centers, international health officials decide which viruses should be included in new flu vaccines.

For influenza, WHO officials also warn countries about the chances of an outbreak. The warning system has different levels of surveillance alert. In the lowest level, a new or an existing flu virus has been found in animals. The risk of humans catching the virus, however, is very low. In the next level up, a few humans have caught the virus from

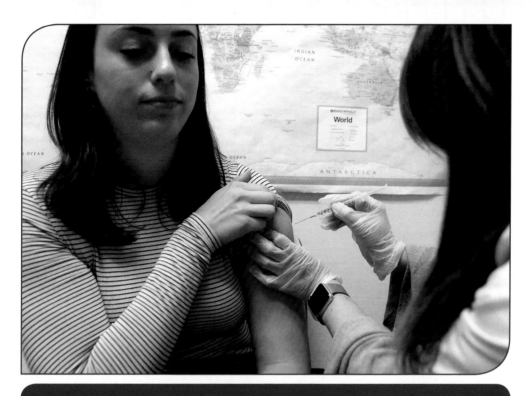

A flu shot, such as the one this woman is receiving, helps to protect against influenza. A new flu vaccine is made every year to combat newly emerging types of flu viruses.

animals, but risk of infection to most people remains low. If more people become infected by contact with animals, then the risk of it spreading from person to person grows. Once the virus is established in humans, the likelihood of a pandemic also grows.

Unlike influenza, some diseases are very difficult to track through organized watch programs. For example, areas of central and western Africa are affected by outbreaks of Ebola virus disease. The first symptoms of this disease include fever, diarrhea, and vomiting. These symptoms are very similar to symptoms of other diseases that are common in Africa. As a result, it is difficult to know right away whether someone is ill with Ebola. In addition, many areas where Ebola is likely to appear have limited ability to closely observe infectious diseases. Because of these challenges, health workers in areas threatened by Ebola are encouraged to contact their country's health authorities as soon as they suspect that a patient is sick with Ebola.

Rapid Response

When an outbreak of disease is detected, health officials must respond swiftly. Among the first to be sent into action is an outbreak response team. An outbreak response team consists of public health experts, epidemiologists (scientists who study how diseases spread and how to control or stop them), an administrative officer, and an environmental health specialist. The team prepares a checklist to assess, or evaluate, an outbreak. Team members gather equipment, such as computers and lab supplies. They organize transport and communication, and they talk to local officials about the outbreak and whether more supplies are needed. Outbreak response teams also investigate cases of illness and carry out contact tracing. Contact tracing is identifying the people who may have come in contact with an infected person. People identified as contacts are watched by doctors until they are no longer contagious. Contacts can remain contagious for days or weeks.

Another key part of the response to a disease outbreak is the quick and accurate collection of information. All sorts of information is needed. For example, the political background of the affected area is very important. Areas struck by an epidemic may also be experiencing violence, war, or political upheaval. It is also necessary to know the health status of the local people. An epidemic may take place in a region where people are affected by other diseases, such as malaria or HIV/AIDS. This situation can affect the speed at which a disease spreads and the degree to which it may make people ill.

Health workers in Seoul, South Korea, wear protective gear as an extra precaution from Middle East respiratory syndrome (MERS). MERS is a dangerous infection of the parts of the body used in breathing. A MERS outbreak took place in South Korea in 2015, prompting an emergency response by public health officials.

Emergency responders visit the affected area on foot. They interview patients and health officials, carry out surveys, and collect data from medical facilities. They may also use a drone or an airplane to gain an aerial perspective of the area. The information that is gathered is used to figure out the extent of the emergency. It is also used to identify groups of people who are at highest risk of infection and who should be treated first.

Defending Against Outbreaks

The best defense against epidemics and pandemics is being prepared. Even with just a small amount of planning ahead, it is possible to save lives when a disease emerges. There are many ways in which countries can prepare. One way includes the stockpiling of vaccines and medicines. Another way is making sure that response teams can gather quickly. Having health workers who can relay information about disease risk to the public and educate people about disease is also important.

Planning Ahead

Epidemics and pandemics require careful planning and preparation. A key part of this preparation is stockpiling. Before an outbreak begins, international, national, and local health agencies gather and maintain stockpiles of medicines and vaccines. Emergency vaccine stockpiles that are kept by international groups help ensure that people in poorer countries can get vaccines when they need them.

Planning ahead for an outbreak also means making sure that people in affected areas can obtain safe, clean food and water. Shelter with proper sanitation, waste disposal, and control of disease-carrying pests, especially mosquitoes, is also necessary. Health workers

A man inspects medical supplies at a warehouse in Alabama. The stockpiling of medical supplies and other activities, such as conducting drills and developing educational materials, are key to lessening the devastation of a disease outbreak.

and individuals who are at high risk of disease exposure may also require the use of personal protection equipment, such as masks, gloves, gowns, and mosquito nets.

International health agencies also have plans in place to deal with specific outbreak scenarios. WHO, for example, has a unique preparedness plan known as the R&D Blueprint. The R&D Blueprint is designed to mobilize research and development activities in the event of an epidemic caused by "disease X." Disease X is any as yet unknown pathogen. Medical, scientific, and regulatory resources provided through Blueprint allow for the fast development of tests to detect new pathogens. These resources also can be used to speed the discovery of medicines and vaccines that can be used against infectious agents.

The Coalition for Epidemic Preparedness Innovations (CEPI) is a global partnership between public and private organizations. The CEPI specializes in the rapid development of vaccines to stop future epidemics. Still other researchers are investigating new technologies to improve existing vaccines. An example is a needle-free measles vaccine that can be inhaled as a powder. This new type of measles vaccine has the potential to eliminate the need for vaccine refrigeration and the use of sterile needles, which can limit the use of the measles vaccine in some places. Scientists are also investigating oral vaccines, which can be taken by mouth, for epidemic diseases. One example is an oral tablet vaccine against norovirus, a highly contagious pathogen that causes diarrhea and vomiting and commonly spreads on cruise ships, in health care facilities, schools and child care centers, and at restaurants and catered events.

Risk Communication Experts

Even before an outbreak begins, individuals known as risk communication experts reach out to the public to help raise awareness of the risk of infectious disease. Their main job is to lay to rest public fears about outbreaks. Risk communication helps people discover ways in which they can reduce their own risk of becoming infected in the event of an epidemic or pandemic. Working together with health officials and disease experts, risk communication experts gather details and facts about the likelihood of an outbreak happening. They learn whether the risk of infection would be high or low and how infection might affect health. They also collect information on things people can do to reduce their own risk of becoming infected. Risk communication experts relay this information to the media and general public in different ways. They often use social media and involve community members.

Understanding Risk

Engaging and communicating with the public is essential to the preparation of disease outbreaks. Educating people in a village, town, or city about communicable diseases and how such diseases spread can help prevent outbreaks. It also can limit the spread of diseases if and when they emerge. Community engagement enables health officials to address individuals' concerns and offer tips about what to do during an outbreak. When equipped with the right information, people are better able to decide how best to protect their health.

Posters such as these, which explain how to protect against Zika virus infection and are presented in different languages, are one way that health officials engage and communicate with the public. Effective communication is essential to the preparation of disease outbreaks.

There are multiple ways in which experts can provide information to people in a community. These include traditional media, such as television, radio, and newspapers, as well as social media. To communicate effectively, health officials must have an understanding of the communities they engage. This awareness includes knowledge of individuals' beliefs and local traditions. Experts must also be able to deal with misinformation and rumor, which can arise when science, technology, or medical practice challenges peoples' beliefs.

Engineering Solutions

Despite much effort to prepare for disease outbreaks, health workers and researchers in many countries still struggle to find diseases and prevent them from spreading. To help these countries improve their health security, WHO, in partnership with other groups, offers a process called joint external evaluation (JEE). JEE is a voluntary and collaborative process. It identifies a country's strengths and weaknesses in terms of its ability to prevent, detect, and respond to disease risks. JEE is very useful for the discovery of gaps in health security. National health officials can then work to fill these gaps. Doing so can result in a more coordinated outbreak action plan, which is important for a quick and effective response.

Many countries have completed JEEs, but few have gone on to develop plans to improve their ability to respond to epidemics. One exception is Tanzania, which used its JEE data to create a national action plan. The country put its new plan to use in 2017 in response to an anthrax outbreak. Outbreaks of anthrax, a disease that is transmitted from livestock to humans, occur frequently in Tanzania. In the past, anthrax cases were underreported, which made containing the disease difficult. Following the development of the country's action plan, however, health workers were able to bring the 2017 outbreak under control quickly. This response was due largely to better collaboration between individuals from different areas of

A Maasai herder in Tanzania cares for his goats. Tanzania set up an action plan during an anthrax outbreak in 2017, which greatly lowered the risk of disease transmission to humans.

expertise and quick decision making by response teams. The training of veterinarians in anthrax control measures also played a role.

To prepare for outbreaks, some countries have also developed real-time, early-alert surveillance systems. For example, in 2014, the Caribbean Public Health Agency (CARPHA), partnering with the Caribbean Tourism Organization, launched the Tourism and Health Programme (THP). The Caribbean economy is heavily dependent on tourism. The movement of travelers in hotels and rental homes and those coming and going from cruise ships, however, greatly increases the risk of food- and water-borne gastrointestinal illness. These illnesses can cause problems for local medical facilities and force businesses to close, causing economic effects. To reduce this damage, health officials decided to raise awareness of food- and water-borne illness among people working in the region's tourism industry. They also identified ways to provide timely alerts of illness to allow for a rapid and coordinated response. CARPHA monitors illnesses that tend to be common among travelers. Through the THP, CARPHA also provides real-time health information for tourists on the internet. In the event of an outbreak, CARPHA officials provide information to cruise ship operators and owners of hotels and other rental properties for guests. Owners and operators can use this information to decide on strategies they can put in place to prevent an outbreak from growing beyond their control.

CHAPTER FOUR

What You Can Do to Prepare

What can you do to prepare for an epidemic or pandemic? To begin with, each person can take care of his or her own natural defenses. These defenses include the skin, which acts as a barrier to infection, and the immune system, which attacks disease agents. Keeping your skin clean will prevent many pathogens from getting into your body. You can do this by washing your hands well every time you go to the bathroom and before eating or preparing food. You can protect your immune system by eating a healthy diet, getting enough sleep, and exercising regularly.

There are many other things each person can also do to bolster his or her protection. Local, national, and international health agencies have identified steps individuals can take to plan ahead for major outbreaks of illness. Being prepared is especially important in the event that health services become unavailable or if someone in your family has special health needs.

Vaccinate

One of the best ways to maximize your protection from existing contagious diseases and new diseases is to make sure you and your family members are up to date on vaccinations. Vaccines against known diseases, including influenza, measles, shingles, and whooping cough, offer protection against those diseases. Vaccination is especially important for young children and the elderly. At first, infants have natural immunity against many diseases thanks to antibodies they received from their mothers. Throughout the first year of life, however, this immunity wears off. While a child's body can still fight off many infectious agents, it may not be able to defend against all of them. Agents such as influenza and polio can have devastating effects. Vaccines help a child's immune system prepare for exposure to these sometimes life-threatening infections. As more children become vaccinated, the diseases they are protected against become less frequent.

The importance of childhood vaccination is illustrated by the measles vaccine. Measles is a highly contagious viral disease. Simply being in the same room with an infected person drastically increases the chances of measles spreading. Infants and young children are especially vulnerable and develop fever, cough, eye irritation, and a rash after becoming infected. Although some people overcome infection without problems, others develop life-threatening complications. The first measles vaccine became available in the 1960s. By 2000, thanks to widespread vaccination of children, the disease was eliminated from the United States. In the following decade, however, increasing numbers of US children were exempted from vaccination. These exemptions, not based on true medical reasons, often were based on the personal beliefs of their parents. Many of these parents believed vaccination was unnecessary or posed health risks. This situation, in addition to the arrival of unvaccinated children from other countries, led to a return of measles. The number of measles outbreaks each year in the United States has grown steadily. According to the US Centers for Disease Control and Prevention (CDC), there were thirty-eight measles outbreaks from 2001 to 2008 and sixty-six outbreaks from 2009 to 2014. The largest of these outbreaks was in 2014, when 383 people fell ill with measles in an Amish community in Ohio. Many people in the community had not been vaccinated against measles.

This boy is fighting a measles infection. Measles is easily prevented through vaccination. The more people who receive the vaccine, the less likely the disease is to infect individuals who cannot undergo vaccination for medical reasons. This protection through widespread vaccination against a disease is known as herd immunity.

Vaccination in elderly people is important, too, because of aging-related declines in their ability to fight off infections. In older persons, a frequent cause of death from new strains of flu is pneumonia. Pneumonia develops when new infections weaken the immune system. Elderly individuals are especially vulnerable to secondary pneumonia. This condition develops when an influenza infection causes the bacteria *Staphylococcus aureus* or *Streptococcus pneumoniae* to travel to the lungs. When this happens, the person develops a second infection called bacterial pneumonia. A vaccine for bacterial pneumonia is available for individuals over age sixty-five. Such vaccinations are a simple and potentially life-saving measure.

Herd Immunity

Herd immunity, or community immunity, is when the number of people in a group who are protected against an infectious agent is very high. When this situation happens, the infectious agent cannot spread easily through the group. Herd immunity can be "caught," or acquired naturally, or may be the result of widespread vaccination. When enough people are able to repel an infection, even those who remain susceptible are less likely to become infected. With fewer and fewer people passing the disease, the disease eventually is eliminated from the population. The vaccination of large numbers of people is considered a safe and effective way of producing herd immunity. For highly contagious infectious agents, such as measles, however, very many individuals must be immune for herd immunity to work. When vaccination rates for a disease dip too low to keep herd immunity, the chances of that disease resurfacing in the group increase significantly.

Stay Smart and Healthy!

Knowledge is one of the best weapons against infectious diseases. Knowing which diseases are threats and understanding their causes, how they spread, and how to protect yourself against them can help keep you safe during an epidemic or pandemic. One of the simplest ways to protect yourself against illness is to wash your hands. According to the CDC, there are five steps to proper handwashing:

1. Use running water to wet your hands. The water can be warm or cold.

2. Use soap and rub the soap into a lather.

3. Scrub vigorously for at least twenty seconds.

4. Rinse thoroughly.

5. Dry your hands using a clean towel or air dry. You can also use the towel to turn the water faucet off.

To reduce the likelihood of spreading infectious agents, it is best to wash your hands after using the restroom. You should also wash hands before, during, and after preparing food and before eating and when caring for someone who is ill. It is also important to wash your hands after blowing your nose or covering your nose or mouth when sneezing or coughing and after touching animal feed and wastes.

Keeping yourself healthy is another way to prevent infections. Getting adequate sleep, eating a healthy diet, getting daily exercise, and managing stress are essential to maintaining personal health. A healthy body has the best chance of fighting off an infection.

Other Measures You Can Take to Prepare

In an emerging crisis, it is always important to make sure that you and your family are well supplied. Your parents may keep stockpiles of some supplies already. A supply of extra food, water, and other essentials is critical. Be sure

An infection control supervisor demonstrates proper handwashing techniques during a field visit to a health clinic in Guinea in Africa. Proper handwashing is one of the simplest ways to protect yourself against illness.

to check the expiration date on products and replace them when needed. You should also understand how to use disinfectants safely and properly and, when outdoors or traveling to areas known to have disease-carrying insects such as mosquitoes, how to properly use insect repellants.

Outbreaks of illness sometimes cause schools to close or force adults to temporarily work from home. Such closures may last only a day or two, but sometimes they can last longer, so you may need to plan activities for home in the event that your school is closed during an outbreak. You may also decide to avoid crowded areas, such as shopping malls.

A person demonstrates the proper application of insect repellant spray. Insect repellants are one way you can protect yourself against bites and stings from disease-carrying insects when outdoors. Wearing long-sleeved shirts and long pants are other ways to prevent insect bites while outside.

Finally, if you are not feeling well, report the symptoms of illness to your parents or caregiver immediately and take precautions, such as wearing a face mask if you develop a cough. Although some infectious illnesses have no specific treatment, it is important to stay hydrated and to get plenty of rest. If your illness can be treated, the sooner you seek care, the more likely you are to have a quick recovery.

Facing Disease in the Twenty-First Century

Engineering solutions to epidemics and pandemics is one of the great challenges of the twenty-first century. In an era of rapid global travel, contagious and potentially deadly infectious diseases

Information Is Key

In the event of an epidemic or pandemic, it is important to keep a list of emergency contacts, with phone numbers, addresses, and information on how to get in touch quickly. Emergency contacts may include family members, neighbors, close friends, or other individuals in your community whom you know and trust. Other contacts include your family doctor, the local or state public health department, your family's pharmacy and hospital, your school, and your parents' employers. It is also important to carry information about your blood type, about medicines that you are taking, and about allergies that you may have to certain foods or drugs. Adults in your family should make sure that they have a way to fill essential prescriptions for relatives with special needs.

can be transported across the world at extraordinary speed. To manage these threats, scientists, medical professionals, and health officials have joined forces, coming up with solutions that bring together concepts that lie at the foundation of STEM education. These experts are making use of advances in science and technology, especially progress in disease surveillance. Disease surveillance, in which experts systematically collect and analyze data and distribute data to public health workers, doctors, and health officials has proven critical to preventing and controlling disease. Thanks to this work, national and international health agencies and individuals are better prepared for epidemics and pandemics than ever before.

Glossary

antibody A substance produced by the immune system that is capable of killing an infectious agent.

anticipate To predict, expect, or foresee.

bacteria (singular bacterium) A type of organism that causes infectious disease.

contact tracing The identification of individuals who may have come in contact with an infected person.

contagious disease An illness transmitted from person to person, typically through sneezing, coughing, or direct contact.

epidemic A sudden occurrence of disease in which the number of cases is higher than what is normal for the affected population.

exempted Excused from or not required to do something.

fatality rate The number of deaths from a particular disease or cause in a specific area.

gastrointestinal Of the stomach and intestines.

herd immunity Also called community immunity, when the number of people able to repel an infectious agent increases to the point that a disease cannot spread easily through a population.

immunity The ability of the body to repel or defend against infection.

infectious disease An illness caused by a microscopic agent, such as a type of bacteria or a virus, that infects the body.

meninges The membranes covering the brain and spinal cord.

mutate To undergo a change.

norovirus A highly contagious infectious agent that causes diarrhea and vomiting. It commonly spreads on cruise ships, in schools and child care centers, in health care facilities, and at restaurants and catered events.

outbreak The sudden appearance of a disease or illness in a group of individuals.

pandemic An epidemic but on a much larger scale, across multiple large countries or worldwide.

pathogen An agent, usually microscopic, such as a virus, that infects the body and causes disease.

patient zero Also called index case, the first carrier or first case of disease in an outbreak.

risk communication The process of making people aware of potential health hazards and how to prepare for exposure to these hazards.

secrete To produce and release a substance.

species A group of living organisms that have similar characteristics to one another and that are able to produce offspring together.

surveillance Keeping close watch, such as watching over the emergence of infectious diseases.

susceptible Having little resistance to something such as a disease.

toxin A poisonous substance that is produced by bacteria, plants, or animals.

trichloroethylene An industrial chemical, vapors from which are a suspected cause of cancer.

vaccine Preparation of a weakened or killed infectious agent or its toxin that provides immunity, or protection, against potentially life-threatening diseases.

virus A microscopic agent that infects cells, a common cause of infectious disease.

For More Information

Centers for Disease for Control and Prevention (CDC)
1600 Clifton Road NE, MS D-25
Atlanta, GA 30333
(800) CDC-INFO (800-232-4636)
Website: https://www.cdc.gov
Facebook: @CDC
Twitter: @CDCgov
The CDC is the health protection agency of the United States,
    playing a critical role in protecting US citizens from health
    threats and saving lives.

Coalition for Epidemic Preparedness Innovations (CEPI)
1901 Pennsylvania Avenue NW, Suite 1003
Washington, DC 20006
Website: https://cepi.net
Twitter: @CEPIvaccines
CEPI is an alliance between public and private groups worldwide
    that finances and coordinates vaccine development as part of
    the larger effort to prevent and contain epidemics.

European Centre for Disease Prevention and Control (ECDC)
Gustav III:s Boulevard 40
169 73 Solna
Sweden
Website: https://www.ecdc.europa.eu
Facebook: @ECDC.EU
Twitter: @ECDC_EU
The ECDC is an agency of the European Union that works to

strengthen Europe's preparedness against outbreaks of infectious disease.

Johns Hopkins Center for Health Security (CHS)
621 East Pratt Street, Suite 210
Baltimore, Maryland 21202
(443) 573-3304
Website: http://www.centerforhealthsecurity.org
Twitter: @JHSPH_CHS
The Johns Hopkins Center for Health Security works to protect
    public health from the effects of epidemics and other health
    disasters.

National Collaborating Centre for Infectious Diseases (NCCID)
Basic Medical Sciences Building, Room L332A
745 Bannatyne Avenue
Rady Faculty of Health Sciences, University of Manitoba
Winnipeg, MB R3E 0W2
Canada
(204) 318-2591
Website: https://nccid.ca
Twitter: @CentreInfection
The NCCID helps connect the public with infectious disease
    science, raising public health awareness.

Pan-Canadian Public Health Network (PHN)
Public Health Agency of Canada
130 Colonnade Road
Ottawa, ON K1A 0K9
Canada
(613) 954-8524
Website: http://www.phn-rsp.ca
PHN is a network of officials across sectors and different levels of

government in Canada that works to strengthen the country's public health.

US Agency for International Development (USAID)
Ronald Reagan Building
Washington, DC 20523-1000
(202) 712-0000
Website: https://www.usaid.gov
Facebook and Twitter: @USAID
USAID is an international development agency based in the
    United States. Among its endeavors is the Emerging Pandemic
    Threats program.

World Health Organization (WHO)
Avenue Appia 20
1202 Geneva
Switzerland
+41-22-7912111
Website: https://www.who.int
Facebook and Twitter: @WHO
WHO serves a leading role in global health responses and in
    directing international health and within the framework of the
    United Nations.

For Further Reading

Canavan, Thomas. *Fighting Illness and Injury: The Immune System.* New York, NY: PowerKids Press, 2015.

Cummings, Judy Dodge. *Epidemics and Pandemics: Real Tales of Deadly Diseases.* North Mankato, MN: Nomad Press, 2018.

Goldsmith, Connie. *Pandemic: How Climate, the Environment, and Superbugs Increase the Risk.* Minneapolis, MN: Twenty-First Century Books, 2019.

Hardyman, Robyn. *The Race to End Epidemics.* New York, NY: Rosen Central, 2015.

Koontz, Robin Michal. *The Science of a Pandemic.* Ann Arbor, MI: Cherry Lake Publishing, 2015.

Laine, Carolee, and Ana S. Ayala. *Ebola Outbreak.* Minneapolis, MN: Essential Library, 2016.

Lewis, Mark L. *Measles: How a Contagious Rash Changed History.* North Mankato, MN: Capstone Press, 2019.

Nardo, Don. *How Vaccines Changed the World.* San Diego, CA: ReferencePoint Press, 2019.

Newman, Patricia. *Ebola: Fears and Facts.* Minneapolis, MN: Millbrook Press, 2016.

Peters, Marilee. *Patient Zero: Solving the Mysteries of Deadly Epidemics.* Toronto, ON: Annick Press, 2014.

Rooney, Anne. *Infectious Diseases.* Mankato, MN: Smart Apple Media, 2012.

Shoals, James. *Epidemics and Pandemics.* Broomall, PA: Mason Crest, 2019.

Spilsbury, Louise. *Health and Disease.* London, UK: Raintree, 2013.

Willett, Edward. *Infectious Disease Specialists: Hunting Down Disease.* New York, NY: Enslow Publishing, 2016.

Bibliography

Ampofo, William K., et al. "Strengthening the Influenza Vaccine Virus Selection and Development Process: Report of the 3rd WHO Informal Consultation for Improving Influenza Vaccine Virus Selection Held at WHO Headquarters, Geneva, Switzerland, 1–3 April 2014." *Vaccine*, August 26, 2015.https://www.sciencedirect.com/science/article/pii/S0264410X15009056.

Bonney, Joseph Humphrey Kofi, et al. "Molecular Detection of Dengue Virus in Patients Suspected of Ebola Virus Disease in Ghana." *PLOS One*, December 19, 2018. https://dx.doi.org/10.1371%2Fjournal.pone.0208907.

Caribbean Public Health Agency (CARPHA). "Caribbean Tourism and Health Programme." Retrieved February 8, 2019. http://carpha.org/What-We-Do/Tourism-and-Health-Programme.

Centers for Disease Control and Prevention (CDC). "Crisis & Emergency Risk Communication (CERC)." Emergency Preparedness and Response. Retrieved January 29, 2019. https://emergency.cdc.gov/cerc.

Centers for Disease Control and Prevention (CDC). "Handwashing: Clean Hands Save Lives." Retrieved February 9, 2019. https://www.cdc.gov/handwashing/index.html.

Gates, Bill. "The Next Epidemic—Lessons from Ebola." *New England Journal of Medicine*, April 9, 2015. https://www.nejm.org/doi/full/10.1056/NEJMp1502918.

Jong, Elaine C., Dennis L. Stevens, and Frank H. Netter. *Netter's Infectious Diseases.* Philadelphia, PA: Elsevier/Saunders, 2012.

Kim, Leesun, et al. "Safety and Immunogenicity of an Oral Tablet Norovirus Vaccine, a Phase 1 Randomized, Placebo-Controlled Trial." *JCI Insight*, July 12, 2018. https://insight.jci.org/articles/view/121077.

Mehand, Massinissa Si, et al. "The WHO R&D Blueprint: 2018 Review of Emerging Infectious Diseases Requiring Urgent Research and Development Efforts." *Antiviral Research*, November 2018. https://www.sciencedirect.com/science/article/pii/S0166354218305643?via%3Dihub.

MVPD Author Group et al. "Safety and Immunogenicity of Dry Powder Measles Vaccine Administered by Inhalation: A Randomized Controlled Phase I Clinical Trial." *Vaccine*, November 28, 2014. https://www.sciencedirect.com/science/article/pii/S0264410X14013620?via%3Dihub.

Nguyen, Hien H. "Influenza Clinical Presentation." Medscape, February 1, 2019. https://emedicine.medscape.com/article/219557-clinical#b3.

Prevent Epidemics. "Tanzania's Lessons Learned—How Assessments Help Them Prepare for Health Threats." Prevent Epidemics, April 11, 2018. https://preventepidemics.org/stories/success-story-2.

Substance Abuse and Mental Health Services Administration. *Key Substance Use and Mental Health Indicators in the United States: Results from the 2017 National Survey on Drug Use and Health* (HHS Publication No. SMA 18-5068, NSDUH Series H-53). Center for Behavioral Health Statistics and Quality, Substance Abuse and Mental Health Services Administration. Retrieved February 6, 2019. https://www.samhsa.gov/data/report/2017-nsduh-annual-national-report.

Tabuchi, Hiroko. "A Trump County Confronts the Administration Amid a Rash of Child Cancers." *New York Times*, January 2, 2019. https://www.nytimes.com/2019/01/02/climate/tce-cancer-trump-environment-deregulation.html.

USAID. "Emerging Pandemic Threats." Retrieved February 6, 2019. https://www.usaid.gov/news-information/fact-sheets/emerging-pandemic-threats-program.

WebMD Medical Reference. "What Are Epidemics, Pandemics, and Outbreaks?" May 11, 2017. https://www.webmd.com /cold-and-flu/what-are-epidemics-pandemics-outbreaks#1.

Wilson, David, and Daniel T. Halperin. "'Know Your Epidemic, Know Your Response': A Useful Approach, If We Get It Right." *The Lancet*, August 9, 2008. https://www.thelancet.com/journals /lancet/article/PIIS0140-6736(08)60883-1/fulltext.

World Health Organization. *A Framework for Global Outbreak Alert and Response.* Department of Communicable Disease Surveillance and Response. Retrieved January 28, 2019. https://www.who.int/csr/resources/publications/surveillance /whocdscsr2002.pdf?ua=1.

World Health Organization. "Joint External Evaluations." Strengthening Health Security by Implementing the International Health Regulations. Retrieved January 28, 2019. https://www.who.int/ihr/procedures/joint-external-evaluations /en.

World Health Organization. "Pandemic Preparedness." Influenza. Retrieved January 28, 2019. https://www.who.int/influenza /preparedness/pandemic/en.

Index

About the Author

Kara Rogers has edited many books and articles on topics in biomedicine and the life sciences. She is the author of *The Quiet Extinction: Stories of North America's Rare and Threatened Plants* (2015) and *Genetic Engineering* (2019) and is a member of the National Association of Science Writers.

Photo Credits

Cover Thomas Coex/AFP/Getty Images; cover hexagons (left to right) Nattapong Wongloungud/EyeEm/Getty Images, CHUYN/E+/Getty Images, D-Keine/E+/Getty Images, © iStockphoto.com/Alessandro Rizzo, john finney photography/Moment/Getty Images, Fernando Ojeda/EyeEm/Getty Images; pp. 4-5 (background) Warchi/iStock/Getty Images; p. 5 (inset) D-Keine/E+/Getty Images; p. 7 Mohammed Hamoud/Getty Images; p. 8 Francisco Leong/AFP/Getty Images; p. 10 BSIP/UIG/Getty Images; p. 12 David McNew/Getty Images; p. 15 Fabrice Coffrini/AFP/Getty Images; p. 17 John Moore/Getty Images; p. 19 Justin Sullivan/Getty Images; p. 21 Bloomberg/Getty Images; p. 23 © AP Images; p. 25 Jeff Greenberg/Universal Images Group/Getty Images; p. 27 SOPA Images/LightRocket/Getty Images; p. 31 CHBD/E+/Getty Images; p. 33 Lindsey Horton/CDC; p. 34 CDC; cover and interior pages graphic elements © iStockphoto.com/koto_feja (spiral design), Ralf Hiemisch/Getty Images (dot pattern).

Design and Layout: Tahara Anderson; Senior Editor: Kathy Kuhtz Campbell; Photo Researcher: Sherri Jackson.